Who We Are

Joe Rhatigan

What Is Culture?

Culture is how we live.
It is our music and foods.
It is our holidays and religions.
It is our languages too.

Americans share the same country.
But they have many different cultures.
That makes the country special.

Jump into Fiction

Ana's First Day

Ana stands in front of the class.
"What is Perú like?" Kyle asks.
"What foods do you eat?"
Stacy asks.
Ana is confused.
Perú is normal.
She eats regular food.

At recess, Ana still feels like the other kids are looking at her oddly.
Then, Kyle says, "Let's play tag!"

Ana smiles.
She loves tag!
Soon, Ana is "It."
She doesn't feel so different anymore.

Back to Nonfiction

We Are Different

The way you live is normal to you.

But it may seem strange to others.

We are all different.

We have our own cultures.

The Games We Play

In the United States, people play tag. In Brazil, it is called *queimada*. Ana would call it *las chapadas*.

People do fun things in their cultures.
They have parties and parades.
They dance and sing.
People eat tasty foods too.

Food Fight!

Buñol is a city in Spain with a fun party. People come from all over to join in. Then, they throw tomatoes at one another!

What about holidays?
Muslims have a big feast in the spring.
Chinese people hang lights in the fall.
Many days are special days somewhere!

Think and Talk

What holidays do you celebrate?

Share What You Know!

People like to share their cultures.
They may post photos and videos.
They may share songs and poems.

The internet helps people share.
It helps people learn about others.

Story Time!

Cultures have their own stories.
They can be silly or scary.
They help people celebrate their cultures.

Differences Are Good

Some people can be mean online or in person.
They might make fun of how others dress or talk.
They might say mean things about what other people do.
Those people can make differences seem strange or scary.

That can change when we know more about other cultures.
Then, we can see how special we all are.
We can see the good in our differences.
We can see how we are the same too!

How to Learn

It is fun to try new things.
You can try new foods and languages.
Ask questions and learn more!

Learning more can change how people see the world.
Things that once seemed strange can be normal.

People are all different.
But we are all human!
We all have feelings.

Celebrating our differences is great!
We can make the world feel safe for everyone.
We can be kind and learn from each other.
We can all be proud to say, "This is who we are!"

Civics in Action

Have a culture fair. Use it to help your classmates learn about each other.

1. Make a poster about you.
2. Bring an object from your home that helps others learn about you.
3. Share the poster and object. Listen to others share as well.